Utterly Gorgeous CARDS

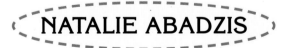

NATALIE ABADZIS

Scholastic Children's Books,
Euston House, 24 Eversholt Street,
London NW1 1DB, UK

A division of Scholastic Ltd
London ~ New York ~ Toronto ~ Sydney ~ Auckland
Mexico City ~ New Delhi ~ Hong Kong

Published in the UK by Scholastic Ltd, 2011

Text by Natalie Abadzis
Illustrations by Natalie Abadzis
Art Director: Liz Standley
Photography by Barry Hayden
Edited by Jo Maggs

ISBN 978 1407 120911

Printed and bound by Tien Wah Press Pte. Ltd, Singapore

2 4 6 8 10 9 7 5 3 1

Utterly Gorgeous Contents

Things you will need

Here's all you need to make a cool collection of Utterly Gorgeous cards!

coloured card and paper

brown paper

black card

cream card

yellow card

orange felt

brown card

blue card

pink card

white card

postcard

cereal box

wrapping paper

striped paper

pinking shears

scissors

hole punch

envelope

shaving foam

newspaper

food colouring

star sequins

tissue paper

pizza box

gold glitter

red glitter

sequins

polystyrene base

sticky tape

glue stick

glitter glue

double-sided tape

pencils

masking tape

ruler

water

thin black pen

thick black pen

felt-tips

paint brushes

matchbox

paper fasteners

fork and spoon

acrylic paint

plastic sleeve

baking tray

ribbon

paint

red ribbon

white ribbon

fabric scraps

gems

cotton thread

silver embroidery thread

peg

5

Dancing shoes

Put on your fanciest dancing shoes and get inspired to make this funky card!

You will need

1 Measure and cut out a piece of colourful card, 30cm x 15cm. Fold it in half, lengthways so you're left with a square card.

2 Draw and cut out two cute shoe shapes from pretty wrapping paper.

Make all kinds of shoes, like chunky, funky trainers!

3 Stick the paper shoes and three little paper hearts onto the front of the card with glue.

4 Cut a few short strands of silver embroidery thread for the shoe laces. Glue them onto the shoes and leave to dry.

Doodle bug

Do you love to doodle?
Use your doodles to make
this quirky card.

1 Use a bright felt-tip
to draw spiral and
flower doodles onto white
card. Then, cut it up into
funky shaped pieces.

2 Arrange the shapes onto
the middle of a piece of
folded card and glue them
down. Simply gorgeous!

Magical motifs

Add charming 'n' cheeky motifs to your cards and stationery to give them tons of personality!

You will need

1 Dab your finger in some paint and splodge rows of fingerprints onto the paper. Leave to dry.

2 Draw simple details onto each splodge with black pen and felt-tips to make them into people, fruit or anything else you like!

Handy tip!
Experiment with different designs and practise your motifs before you use them!

Make sweet l'il motifs from card to add to your stationery, too. They could have a theme to match your letters or cards, like holidays, or just be totally random!

9

Cool closet cards

Make super-cute wardrobe cards for your fashion-crazy friends! Let's get started…

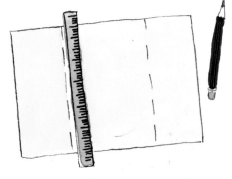

1 Measure and cut out a piece of card, 21cm x 15cm. Measure 5cm in from each edge and draw a line.

2 Fold along both lines using a ruler to help you keep them straight. These flaps are the wardrobe doors.

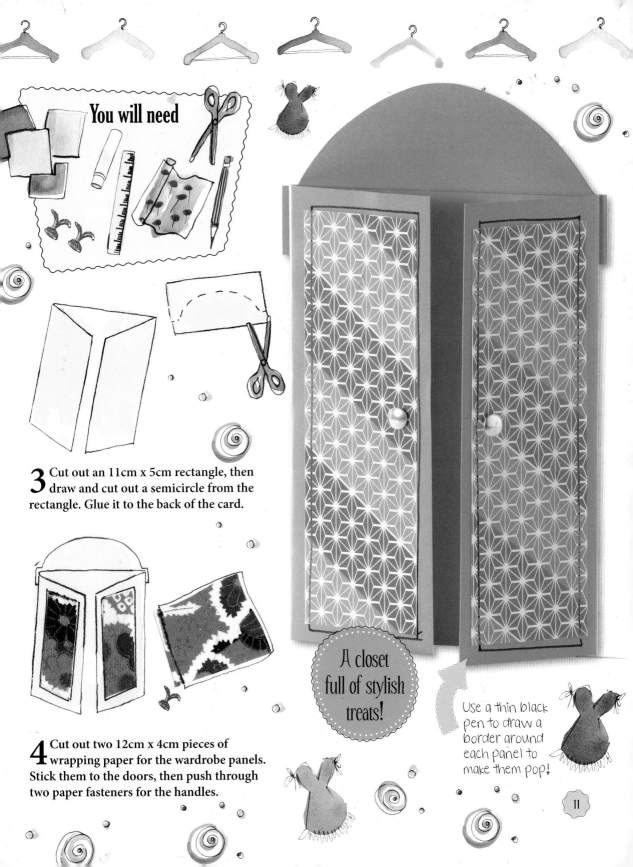

3 Cut out an 11cm x 5cm rectangle, then draw and cut out a semicircle from the rectangle. Glue it to the back of the card.

4 Cut out two 12cm x 4cm pieces of wrapping paper for the wardrobe panels. Stick them to the doors, then push through two paper fasteners for the handles.

A closet full of stylish treats!

Use a thin black pen to draw a border around each panel to make them pop!

11

Whimsical watercolours

You will need

Create dreamy, watercolour patterns and use them as decoration for cards.

Dotty wash

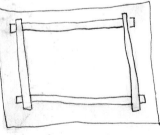

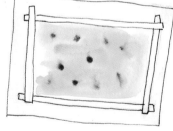

1 Place a piece of paper onto some thick cardboard and stick down the edges with masking tape. Dip your paintbrush in water and brush onto the paper.

2 Paint a yellow wash of colour over the dampened paper. Then dab pink dots over the top. Leave to dry. Totally dreamy!

Pretty rainbow wash

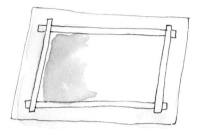

1 Stick a piece of paper to cardboard with masking tape. Dip your paintbrush in water and brush some water onto the paper.

Rockin' rainbow colours!

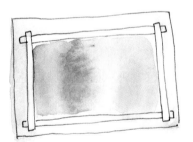

2 Paint one stripe of colour, then paint another colour right next to it so that the edges blend together. Carry on until you have a beautiful rainbow wash.

Make your brush strokes large and loose and have fun with it!

Sweet tweets

Send a sweet tweet treat to someone special with this chirpy little picture card.

1 Fold a 24cm x 18cm piece of card in half. Then cut out a 8cm x 9cm piece of striped paper and glue it to the front.

You will need

Look out of your window to see if you can spot any cute birds!

4 Use a felt-tip to draw legs on the bird, then stick on a sparkly sequin eye!

Make lots in different colours and patterns!

2 Draw a bird and a wing shape onto wrapping paper and cut them out. Then cut out a branch shape from contrasting paper.

3 Stick the bird onto orange felt and cut it out, leaving a border. Then stick the wing to the bird and the bird and branch to the front of the card.

Wish you were here...

Use scraps of fabric and
bits 'n' pieces to make cute,
collaged postcards!

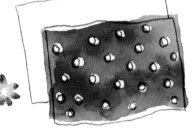

1 Cover the front of a postcard
with some pretty wrapping
paper and stick it on.

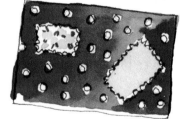

2 Cut out a piece of scrap fabric
and a piece of brown paper
with pinking shears. Glue them
to the front of the postcard.

Handy tip!

If you don't have pinking shears just use regular scissors!

3 Cut pieces of pretty ribbon and stick them onto the postcard so that they overlap the fabric and brown paper.

Design more postcards with other scrap fabric and ribbons!

Quirky handmade postcards!

4 Use a pencil to draw a frame on the brown paper, then stick on three star sequins for a little glitz!

Sassy stripes

Create a striking look with simple stripes. Here's what to do…

Sensationally stripy!

You will need

1 Measure and cut out a piece of card, 16cm x 14cm and fold it in half, lengthways.

Draw patterns, like these cute hearts, onto plain stripes using colourful pens. Adorable!

2 Cut out three, slightly curvy, strips of colourful paper. Stick them onto the right side of the front of the card, then trim the edges down to fit.

3 Cut a few thinner strips of wrapping paper and stick them inside the colourful paper strips.

Handbag honey

Get gorge 'n' girly with these cute-as-you-like handbag cards!

You will need

1 Fold a piece of pretty, card neatly in half.

2 Fold two pieces of colourful paper in half. Draw two 7cm x 4cm rectangles and cut them out. Then cut out a handbag shape from each one.

Handy tip!
You could make mini suitcase, satchel or rucksack shapes, too!

3 Draw little cherries and hearts, or another pretty print, onto the bag shapes with felt-tips.

4 Wrap a loop of 36cm long ribbon around each handbag and stick into place. Then stick the handbags to the front of your card.

Fairy fun

Do you believe in fairies? We do! Here's how to make your own magical fairy cards…

You will need

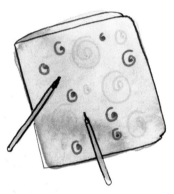

1 Fold a 26cm x 14cm piece of card in half and round off the edges. Use felt-tips the same colour as the card to draw pretty swirls on the front.

2 Draw a circle onto colourful paper and sketch a little face on it. Then draw and cut out some hair from black paper and stick it around the face.

Handy tip!
Put two or three fairies together on one card. Super-sweet!

3 Draw a triangle onto red paper, then round off the edges. Wrap and stick a piece of ribbon around the triangle. This will be the fairy's dress.

Instead of swirls, you could draw stars, dots or other patterns!

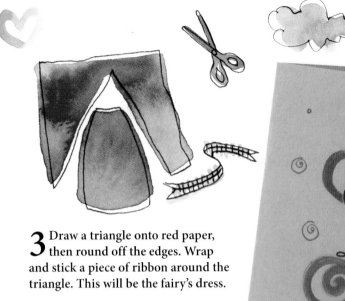

4 Arrange and stick the fairy face and dress to the front of the card. Then draw on arms and legs in black pen. Why not make paper flowers in another colour and stick them on, too?

Fruit, fabulous fruit!

Feast your eyes on this fruity little notelet card. Totally mouthwatering!

Good enough to eat!

1 To make the card sleeve, measure and cut out two pieces of card, 10cm x 7cm. Round off the corners, then stick the two long edges together with double-sided tape.

2 To make the notelet card to slide inside the sleeve, measure and cut out a piece of card, 9cm x 5cm.

4 Use a thick black pen to add an outline to the pineapples and to add a hand drawn border to the notelet card. Now slide the notelet inside the sleeve!

3 Use felt-tips to draw little pineapples on the sleeve. Draw a crisscross pattern on the yellow bodies and green leaves on top. Draw one on the notelet card to match.

Try other cute fruits, like raspberries and strawberries!

Handy tip!
Try using the finger painting technique from page 9 to make your funky fruit patterns!

Retro cuteness

Make a cool collection of retro picture cards, starting with this lovely little lamp!

1 Fold a 26cm x 18cm piece of card in half. Cut out a smaller piece of paper in a different colour and stick it on the front.

You will need

Handy tip!

Why not make other gorgeous images, like a rain coat or a cute pair of wellies?

2 Cut out a small square and two small rectangles for the base of the lamp. Stick them onto the bottom of the card.

3 Cut out a big pink square and a smaller rectangle for the lampshade. Stick them on top of the base.

4 Use a black pen to draw an outline around the border and lamp and some slightly wonky lines across the lampshade for a super-chic look!

27

Tea-party time

These tasty invitations are perfect for organizing totally fun tea parties!

You will need

1 Measure and cut out a piece of brown card 15cm x 10cm and fold it in half, lengthways.

2 To make a cupcake stamp, draw a cupcake onto a polystyrene pizza base in pencil. Make sure you press into the base hard. Cut the stamp out.

3 Dab paint onto the cupcake stamp, then press it down onto a small square of white card for a fab print! Leave to dry.

Take some time for tea & cake!

4 Cut two mini strips of masking tape and use them to stick your print to the front of the brown card. Now your invitation is ready to send!

Cool collage

Get cutting, painting and sticking to create a mega-cool, thrown-together look.

1 Brush yellow and green paint over a 25cm x 15cm piece of white card. Leave to dry, then fold it in half.

2 Paint blocks of pink, black and yellow paint onto some scrap card. Leave to dry.

Cut out shapes to make other pictures, like these funky headphones.

Paint a few cheeky paw prints inside.

3 Draw and cut out some bricks from the pink, a cat from the black and a moon from the yellow. Arrange and stick them onto the card.

4 Outline the bricks with a black pen and make eyes for the cat from white and black card to finish if off.

Utterly fluttery

Fly away with these super-pretty and delicate butterflies. Here's how to make yours…

1 Fold a piece of 21cm x 15cm cream card in half. Round off the corners. Then, fold pieces of pink, red and orange A4 paper in half.

2 Draw one half of a set of butterfly wings along the folded edges of the paper and then a smaller set. Cut them out and unfold the shapes.

Make tiny butterfly confetti following steps 1 and 2!

Then make a little wallet from tissue paper to keep the confetti in.

Fabulous flutterby fun!

3 Layer and stick the butterflies on top of each other at a slight angle, so you can see all of the colours.

4 Arrange and stick the butterflies to the front of your card. Then add delicate details with a black pen.

Funky pop-ups

Surprise your buddies with these super-fun, pop-up pictures.

glue tab

glue tab

glue tab

tuck-in tab

3cm

3cm

glue tab

tuck-in tab

tuck-in tab

tuck-in tab

1 Copy the picture above to make an outline for your box and cut it out. Fold it along the lines, then tuck and stick the tabs into place.

34

You will need

Pop-up flower power!

2 Cut out one yellow 3cm x 30cm strip of card and one blue. Place the ends together at a right angle and fold them up to make a long spring. Stick it inside the box.

3 To make the mini stereo, cut out a wonky rectangle of red card, two yellow circles for the speakers, a mini pink rectangle for the tape deck and a handle shape from blue card. Stick them together.

4 Fold the bottom edge of the stereo underneath to make a tab, then glue the tab to the top of the spring. Now, decorate the box with funky musical notes in black pen!

Monochrome magic

Black and white is an eye-popping combo – so get busy with these mega-cool, monochrome cutouts!

You will need

1 Measure and cut out a piece of black card 24cm x 12cm and fold it in half.

2 Sketch a heart shape onto the front of the card in pencil.

Show the shape of your heart!

Funky flowers are a fun look to try out, too.

3 Carefully score the heart shape with a pair of scissors and cut it out. You might need an adult to help you with this.

4 Cut a piece of white card, 12cm x 12cm and stick it inside the front of the card using double-sided tape.

Lovely l'il lanterns

Light up the front of a card
with some awesome l'il
lanterns. So cute!

1 Cut a piece of card 21cm x 15cm.
Then, fold it in half and turn it
on its side.

2 To make the lanterns,
cut out small rectangles of
colourful paper and fold them
up concertina-style.

*Cut your
colourful paper
into different
sized pieces for a
cool effect!*

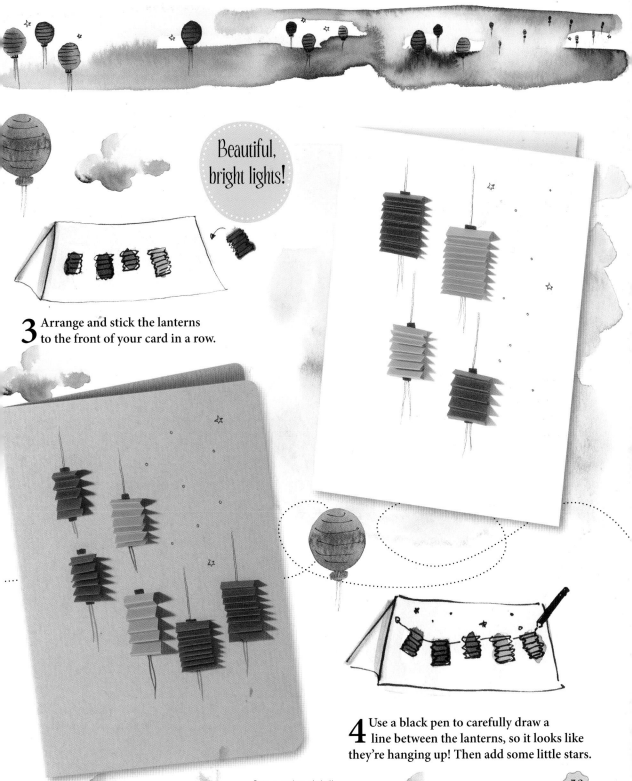

Beautiful, bright lights!

3 Arrange and stick the lanterns to the front of your card in a row.

4 Use a black pen to carefully draw a line between the lanterns, so it looks like they're hanging up! Then add some little stars.

Draw extra detail with bright coloured felt-tips!

Super stencils

Create kooky, layered prints with this stunning stencil technique!

1 Fold a 19cm x 12cm piece of blue card in half, lenghtways. Then cut out a 10cm x 8cm piece of orange card.

2 To make a fan stencil, use a black pen to draw small fan shapes onto a plastic sleeve, then cut them out.

40

Handy tip!
Wipe your plastic stencil clean after each layer of paint.

Make more pretty stencil shapes, like hearts, stars and squares!

3 Place the stencil over the orange card, and tape to a flat surface. Dab gold paint over the fan shapes, then carefully lift the stencil up. Leave to dry, then stencil pink fans over the top at a slight angle.

4 Stick the orange card to the front of the blue card and add cute details to the fans with a black pen.

Window wonder

Send a sweet valentine with a difference and keep your heart in suspense!

You will need

1 Fold a 21cm x 15cm piece of card in half. Draw a 6cm-wide heart in the middle of the card and cut it out.

2 Use felt-tips to draw a border around the edge of the card and vertical stripes onto the front.

Super stars & happy hearts!

3 Draw and cut out a smaller heart from pink card, then glue it to the middle of a length of ribbon.

4 Stick a sparkly gem to the little heart. Stick the ends of the ribbon inside the card, behind the cut out, so that the small heart sits in the big heart window!

Try out other fun patterns, like crazy crosshatch!

Crafty marbling

Find out how to make dreamy, marble-print paper, then use it to make fab flowers!

You will need

1 Squirt some shaving foam into a baking tray. Then add a few drops of food colouring and mix with a fork. Smooth it over with a spoon.

2 Lay a piece of white paper on top and gently press down. Peel it off and lay it on newspaper. Use a spoon to scoop off any excess foam and leave it to dry.

A gorge wild-flower effect!

3 Fold an 18cm x 14cm piece of card into three sections. Draw and cut out flowers from your marble print and stick them across the top of the card. Use a green felt-tip to add the stems!

Ice-cream dream

Use a super-simple tearing technique to make this tasty-lookin' treat!

You will need

1 Measure and cut a piece of card 21cm x 14cm and fold it in half. Round the corners off.

2 Tear up three chunks of colourful paper and stick them to the front of card to make bright background.

3 Tear a piece of orange paper into a triangle for the cone and a gold piece of paper for the edge of the cone and stick them to the card.

4 Lastly, tear up three semicircle shapes for the blobs of ice cream and a long strip for the flake and glue them on.

Dress it up

You will need

Add a touch of elegance to your card collection with these stylish little dresses.

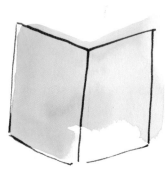

1 Cut out a piece of green card 21cm x 15cm and fold it in half, lengthways.

2 Cut out a piece of orange paper with one wavy edge and stick it to the bottom of the card.

Handy tip!

Sreatch the dresses onto the back of the wrapping paper.

3 Sketch two dresses, roughly 6cm x 3cm, onto wrapping paper and cut them out. Arrange them on the front of the card and stick down.

You could make cute tops and shirts, too!

4 Use a black pen to add outlines and frills to the bottom of each dress and a line at the top of the wave.

Diner delights

Dreamy, diner delicacies
make for a cool, retro card,
so let's get decorating!

1 Fold a piece of A4 paper in half to make an A5 card.

POP CORN

2 Cut out a piece of spotty paper with one wavy edge – this will be the tablecloth. Then cut out a zigzag shape from brown and blue paper and stick it to the top of the card.

3 Sketch two tall ice-cream glasses and two blobs of ice cream onto colourful paper and cut them out.

Handy tip!
Make the yummy cherries from red card and glitter!

Try making a gorge gingham tablecloth for a different card.

4 Arrange and stick your delish ice-cream sundaes onto the card, on top of the spotty tablecloth. Then add glittery red cherries and a straw!

Pretty as a picture

Recreate a gorgeous blossom wall hanging with pretty pastel tissue paper.

1 Fold a piece of 20cm x 15cm white card in half. Then, use a black pen to draw the ends of a wall hanging onto the front.

2 Fold up blue and pink tissue paper and roughly cut out some thin strips.

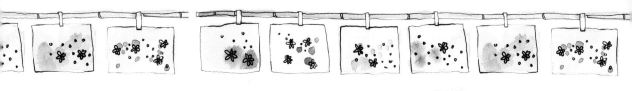

3 Stick some double-sided tape between the ends of the wall hanging on your card. Then stick on the strips of tissue paper, layering them up as you go along.

Handy tip!

Decorate more cards with any leftover tissue paper flowers!

4 Cut out little flowers from tissue paper and stick them over the top randomly. Super-cute!

Ultra-girly gorgeness!

See if you can find some real petals to add to your picture!

Going dotty

Use this dotty, spotty method to make a cheerful cherry, balloon or fairy-light print.

1 Fold a 21cm x 15cm piece of card in half, lengthways. Punch a hole through the the top right corners of the card.

2 Push a loop of 15cm long ribbon through both holes, then push the ends through the loop to secure.

You will need

Use the same technique to make a bright, multi-coloured balloon print!

3 Dip the end of a pencil eraser into red paint and use it to dot pairs of red circles onto the card. Leave to dry.

4 Use felt-tips to add little stalks and leaves and make the circles into adorable cherries!

Marvellous mini books

Hide secret messages for your pals inside these adorable mini-book box cards!

Hide your secret notes in here!

1 Wrap double-sided tape around three sides of the matchbox case. Stick a piece of wrapping paper around it and cut down to size.

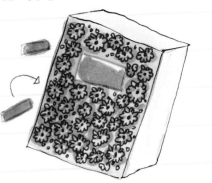

2 Make a little orange label for the front and some tiny rectangle labels for the spine and stick them on with glue.

Make lots in different colours and patterns and line them up for a busy bookshelf effect!

4 Use a black pen to draw borders inside the labels and lines along the top, side and bottom of the box to look like book pages.

Handy tip!

Experiment with fabric covers and different sized boxes!

3 Place the matchbox tray onto some orange paper and draw around it. Cut out the shape and glue inside the tray. Slide it back inside the matchbox.

Invitation only

Roll up, roll up! Find out how to make a stunning set of skate-themed invitations!

You will need

1 Measure and cut out a piece of card, 22cm x 8cm and fold it in half. Make a card for each person you want to invite.

2 Measure and cut out a piece of card, 11cm x 8cm. Then cut out a 10cm x 7cm piece of wrapping paper and stick it to the front.

Party!

RSVP

Party!

Make your invitations in lots of different colour combinations!

RSVP

Handy tip!
Trace over this picture to help you draw your rollerskate.

3 Use the template on this page to help you draw a rollerskate onto wrapping paper. Cut it out and stick to the front of the card from step 1.

4 Add a little glitter-glue star to the skate and one to the card inside. Cut a small piece of card and write the letters 'RSVP' onto it. Glue this to the card inside.

You will need

Notelet sleeves

Here's all you need to make decorative sleeves for your nifty note cards!

1 Fold a piece of wrapping paper in half and cut out a 13cm x 10cm rectangle. Stick the short edges together with double-sided tape.

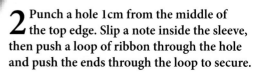

2 Punch a hole 1cm from the middle of the top edge. Slip a note inside the sleeve, then push a loop of ribbon through the hole and push the ends through the loop to secure.

Heart and star spray

Draw a spray on the back of your envelopes, too!

You will need

Draw a spray of tiny hearts and stars across one edge of some plain cards and matching plain envelopes. Super cute!

Elegant envelopes

Give your envelopes a totally unique twist by lining them with gorge, wrapping paper!

You will need

1 Lay your envelope out and open up the flap.

2 Place the open envelope on top of a sheet of wrapping paper, then draw around it.

Try other gorge print and colour combos!

Perfectly pretty post!

4 Now stick the wrapping-paper shape inside your envelope with glue for a super-lovely lining!

3 Draw an outline 1cm from the edge of the envelope shape with a pencil and cut it out.

This makes the shape smaller so that it will easily tuck inside the envelope.

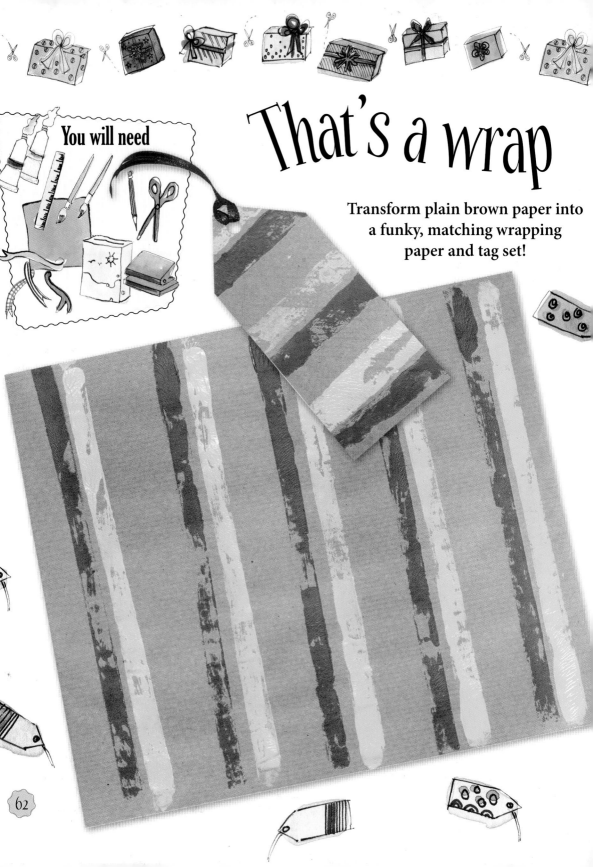

That's a wrap

Transform plain brown paper into a funky, matching wrapping paper and tag set!

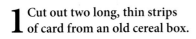

1 Cut out two long, thin strips of card from an old cereal box.

2 Dab red paint onto one strip. Use it to print stripes onto one big and one small piece of brown paper. Leave to dry.

Try other print patterns like polka dots or chunky stripes!

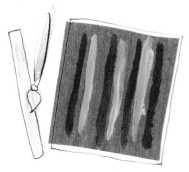

3 Paint the other strip with yellow paint and print yellow stripes in between the red ones. Leave to dry again.

4 Draw and cut out tag shapes from the small piece of stripy paper. Punch a hole through the end of each tag, then push a loop of colourful ribbon through the hole.

Postcard perfection

Personalize the back of your
postcards with gorge sprays and
motif decorations!

You will need